Firmly Planted

Family Study Guide

Firmly Planted: Family Study Guide
God Creates the World and Chooses a Family

Published by
Real Life Press
P.O. Box 1767
Battle Ground, WA 98604

www.firmlyplantedfamily.com
www.firstclasshomeschool.org
www.thebusyhomeschoolmom.com

ISBN: 0-9844323-9-6

Printed in the United States of America

Cover Design by Christi Gifford
www.thegraphiclady.com

Original Art/Graphics by
Savannah St. John Bates & Caylin Floyd
©2012 All Rights Reserved

All Biblical quotations are from the English Standard Version,
New American Standard Bible, King James Version,
New International Version and the Message.

CONTENTS

Note from Heidi and Jay St. John 1

Firmly Planted Icons: Family Study Guide. 3

Week 1 - God Creates the Universe 5

Week 2 - God Creates Humans 12

Week 3 - The Fall 17

Week 4 - Noah and the Flood 23

Week 5 - The Tower of Babel 29

Week 6 - The Call of Abram 35

Week 7 - Isaac on the Altar. 41

Week 8 - Jacob, Rachel and Leah 48

Week 9 - God Wrestles with Jacob 56

Week 10 - The Twelve Sons of Jacob. 61

A Note from Jay & Heidi St. John, Founders of Firmly Planted and First Class Homeschool Ministries

Welcome to the first book in a series of family Bible study resources that we are calling *"Firmly Planted"*.

In Psalm 1:3, the Psalmist David says, "Blessed is the man who trusts in the Lord; he is like a tree, firmly planted by streams of water who yields its fruit in due season and whose leaf does not wither. Whatever he does prospers."

As parents, this is our heart's desire: that our families would be *"Firmly Planted"* in the fertile soil of God's Word, and that as families, we would become students of the Bible. We are told in Timothy that the Bible should be our primary reference tool for life—that "All Scripture is God-breathed and is useful for teaching, rebuking, correcting and training in righteousness, so that the servant of God may be thoroughly equipped for every good work." (2 Timothy 3:16-17 NIV)

While our children are in our care, we have an opportunity to shape their hearts and minds for the Lord. We have an opportunity to teach our children to be amazed by God's creativity as evidenced through His creation. And we have the chance to walk with God in a way that allows our children to grow right along with us.

These books have been designed with that kind of "growing" in mind. We have written *Firmly Planted* with the whole family in mind. The goal is to get families in the Word together! As you begin *Firmly Planted*, you will notice that each lesson features activities and questions for every age group, including coloring pages for little ones, puzzles that reinforce key words and Biblical truths and more thought provoking questions for older students.

Firmly Planted has been designed to assist parents in studying the Bible with their children. Keep in mind that it's not necessarily the quantity of time you spend in God's Word each day. It's the consistency you demonstrate in your commitment to spend time regularly in the Bible together.

Of all the things we have done with our seven children, the time we have spent together in the Word has proven to yield the best fruit. That's because the real "fruit" we desire to see in our children will never be found apart from a growing relationship with Jesus Christ.

Our prayer for you as parents is that you would grow deeper in your walk with the Lord, and in your understanding of His great love for you. Pass it on to your children. Talk about it when you rise up, when you lie down and when you walk along the way. Learn all you can about God and His Word.

It's the best thing you'll ever do together as a family.

Jay & Heidi St. John

Firmly Planted Icons: Family Study Guide

Each component of the Firmly Planted program has it's own symbol. In this way, you can easily see when you finish one section and are starting a new one. The symbols are found throughout the Family Study Guides and the Workbooks.

The Seed

This is the 'big idea' or 'key concept' for the week. (Whenever possible this will always point toward Jesus as revealed and foreshadowed from Genesis to Revelation).

Planting the Seed

This is the Scripture memorization component and might be a simplified 6-12 words for ages 4-11 and a longer 15-25 words for ages 12-18.

Additional Planting the Seed

This is the Scripture memorization component for older kids. More verses, more challenge!

Watering the Seedling

This is the 5-6 minute object lesson for co-ops that helps the seed concept 'germinate' for the student. It's also the icon for "Upper Class", *Firmly Planted's* questions that are geared toward older students.

Daily Study

This is the daily devotion designed to be done with your family. It guides you and your family in a deeper exploration of what God is teaching us in each week's passage.

God Creates the Universe

Genesis 1:1-25

[1] In the beginning, God created the heavens and the earth. [2] The earth was without form and void, and darkness was over the face of the deep. And the Spirit of God was hovering over the face of the waters.

[3] And God said, "Let there be light," and there was light. [4] And God saw that the light was good. And God separated the light from the darkness. [5] God called the light Day, and the darkness he called `[14] And God said, "Let there be lights in the expanse of the heavens to separate the day from the night. And let them be for signs and for seasons, and for days and years, [15] and let them be lights in the expanse of the heavens to give light upon the earth." And it was so. [16] And God made the two great lights—the greater light to rule the day and the lesser light to rule the night—and the stars. [17] And God set them in the expanse of the heavens to give light on the earth,[18] to rule over the day and over the night, and to separate the light from the darkness. And God saw that it was good.[19] And there was evening and there was morning, the fourth day.

[20] And God said, "Let the waters swarm with swarms of living creatures, and let birds fly above the earth across the expanse of the heavens." [21] So God created the great sea creatures and

every living creature that moves, with which the waters swarm, according to their kinds, and every winged bird according to its kind. And God saw that it was good.²² And God blessed them, saying, "Be fruitful and multiply and fill the waters in the seas, and let birds multiply on the earth." ²³ And there was evening and there was morning, the fifth day.

²⁴ And God said, "Let the earth bring forth living creatures according to their kinds—livestock and creeping things and beasts of the earth according to their kinds." And it was so. ²⁵ And God made the beasts of the earth according to their kinds and the livestock according to their kinds, and everything that creeps on the ground according to its kind. And God saw that it was good.

The Seed

God created everything from nothing: the earth, the heavens, light, water, plants and animals.

Planting the Seed

¹ In the beginning, God created the heavens and the earth. Genesis 1:1 **ESV**

Additional Planting the Seed (Ages 11+)

¹ In the beginning was the Word, and the Word was with God, and the Word was God. ² He was in the beginning with God. ³ All things were made through him, and without him was not any thing made that was made. John 1:1-3 **ESV**

Watering the Seedling

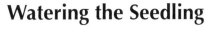

Can you imagine a time that was before—a time before there were animals, before there were stars, before there were oceans or light or even before there was an Earth itself? The Bible begins by telling us that there was such a time. There was a time when there was nothing except for God Himself.

God the Father, Jesus the Son and the Holy Spirit existed before anything else existed. They existed forever.

Then one day something extraordinary happened. God spoke! The voice of God reverberated across time and nothingness, speaking into existence things that existed only in God's creative imagination until that moment.

God said, "Light!" and suddenly light existed and the darkness was overwhelmed by God's light. God studied the light He had just spoken into existence the way a painter might stand back and study his painting and God liked what He saw. It was good.

God continued speaking, His creative voice making something out of nothing. God spoke the sky into being and then He separated His beautiful new sky from the waters below by the power of His voice. He spoke again saying "Earth, come forth!" and the planet we live on was formed as God's voice echoed across the universe.

God looked at the sky, the waters and the Earth and He was delighted with what he saw, but God wasn't finished yet. He spoke again, "Plants, spring up!" and suddenly all manner of trees and flowers, grass and shrubs sprung into being for the first time ever. Beautiful green covered the dull, brown earth and God was pleased with all He saw.

God imagined the waters He had created filled with swimming creatures of every sort: whales and dolphins, eels and sharks, porpoises and sailfish. And as he spoke the words, "Let there be fish!" the ocean was alive with swarming life of every shape, size and color.

Then God spoke once more, "Birds, appear!" and suddenly the sky was filled with beautiful birds of every variety. Think of all the beautiful birds you've ever seen: peacocks and penguins, eagles and doves, cuckoos and pelicans, chickens and robins. They all appeared for the very first time in response to God's creative command.

But God still wasn't finished. He thought for a moment and spoke once more, "Life!" And even before the sound of God's voice died away the earth sprang forth with every living creature you can imagine: zebras and elephants, snakes and orangutans, horses and rabbits, skunks and cows. And God liked what he saw and He gave them all permission to reproduce and multiply and fill the earth that He had created.

Isn't that amazing? We can make things with Play-Doh™ and we can color pictures with Crayons™, but only God can speak something into existence using nothing but His will. His creativity has no limits. He could have created one kind of tree and one kind of bird and one kind of fish and one kind of animal. But instead His creative imagination created millions and millions of species — each one unique and each one created by God's limitless voice.

All of the things we see and enjoy every day in nature exist because God decided they should exist. And nothing in nature exists that He didn't think ought to exist. The sky and the clouds, the rain and the oceans, the birds and the animals, the flowers and the trees-everything that makes up our world was created from nothing by the creative and infinite imagination of God the Father, Jesus the Son and the Holy Spirit. Isn't God good? Isn't He amazing?

 ## Daily Study

Day 1

Before you open up God's Word and begin to talk about it with your family, stop for a moment and ask the Lord to calm everyone from their many daily tasks and busy duties. Take this moment to pray together and ask the Lord to bring His encouragement to your family as they hear His word. Ask for His help to hear His heart in the words and ideas.

Now, re-read the verses that were read in chapel, Genesis 1:1-25. Or if you have very young children try Genesis 1:1 & 2. Read it slowly, thoughtfully, and encourage your whole family to listen joyfully to the incredible "one of a kind" story that is beginning to unfold!

Yes, "beginning"...that is the word!

Next, initiate a conversation that includes the elements in our first question. Gently interact with your family, exploring the heart of God revealed in His words. Ask and listen as different members of your family bring their thoughts as well as their questions.

Here is your question for today:

What do you think the phrase "in the beginning" means?

Who and what do you think existed 'before' that beginning?

Day 2

Read: Genesis 1:1-8 and Genesis 1:14-19

What a joy to ponder the very creation of the universe! Each treasured part of creation: God spoke... and they were! Obviously the heavens declare His glory.

Do we want to know how creative, vast and wonderful God is? Go out often with your family in the evening and look up at the myriad stars! Go out with your family in the day and ponder the power of the sun. The God who made it (and many more stars both larger and smaller than our own sun) is more powerful than all of the stars or suns in the universe! And He is the God who loves us! Yes, you can jump up and down for that!

Now together with your family talk about the ideas below in our question for the day:

What do you think the "lights" were that God created in the expanse of the heavens?

How are those heavenly lights for "signs and for seasons, and for days and years.

Day 3

Do something a little different today. Read out loud the verses from Genesis 1:1 all the way to Genesis 1:25. Listen to all the verses and then ask this question:

What verse made an impression on you? Why? What did it say that made you think?

Afterwards, spend a few moments thanking the Lord. There are so many things that you might be thankful for.

Day 4

Go back and read Lesson 1 again in your *Firmly Planted Family Study Guide* and then sit quietly for a minute or two and think about what this week's lesson tells you about the nature of God. Let different family members contribute various attributes of God that they see in this lesson or have been impressed by.

(Here are some ideas that you might hear: His creativity, His Power, His precision, His perfection, and the fact that He loves things that are good — things that have beauty and purpose.)

After you've enjoyed talking together about how astounding the Lord is, then thank Him for his amazing creation!

God Creates Humans

Genesis 1:26-31

26 Then God said, "Let us make man in our image, after our likeness. And let them have dominion over the fish of the sea and over the birds of the heavens and over the livestock and over all the earth and over every creeping thing that creeps on the earth."

27 So God created man in his own image, in the image of God he created him; male and female he created them.

28 And God blessed them. And God said to them, "Be fruitful and multiply and fill the earth and subdue it, and have dominion over the fish of the sea and over the birds of the heavens and over every living thing that moves on the earth."29 And God said, "Behold, I have given you every plant yielding seed that is on the face of all the earth, and every tree with seed in its fruit. You shall have them for food. 30 And to every beast of the earth and to every bird of the heavens and to everything that creeps on the earth, everything that has the breath of life, I have given every green plant for food." And it was so. 31 And God saw everything that he had made, and behold, it was very good. And there was evening and there was morning, the sixth day.

The Seed

God created man and woman in His own image.

 ## Planting the Seed

²⁷ God created man in his own image.
Genesis 1:27a **ESV**

Additional Planting the Seed
(Ages 11+)

²⁶ Then God said, "Let us make man in our
image, after our likeness."
²⁷ So God created man in his own image,
in the image of God he created him;
male and female he created them.
²⁸ And God blessed them.
Genesis 1:26a, 27, 28a **ESV**

 ## Watering the Seedling

After God finished creating the sky, the
earth, the oceans and all the birds, fish and
animals He still wasn't finished. He had
something else in mind. He wanted to create
something to crown His beautiful creation and to take
charge of His earth. So God the Father, Jesus the Son
and the Holy Spirit came up with their greatest idea yet:
they created man and woman.

God said, "Let us create man in our image, after our
likeness."

Did you know you were created in the image of God?
Isn't that amazing? We each bear the likeness of God
on our soul — created in His image.

What do you suppose it means to be created in the image of God?

God is creative. We saw that in verses 1-25 of Genesis 1, didn't we? And so God made us to be creative too. We can create music and art, write poetry and books. We can plant beautiful gardens and tell wonderful stories. In that way we have one of the many characteristics of God. We're creative.

The Bible tells us in John 10:11 that Jesus is the Good Shepherd. And we were created to be good shepherds too. God tells us that He has given us all of the plants, fish, birds and animals for our enjoyment and use. Isn't that what a shepherd does? A shepherd takes charge of the sheep and looks after them. So that's another way we're created in God's image. We're shepherds!

Also, God is eternal. Before anything else existed, God was there. And God will live forever. He has no end. And we too were created to live forever — in the image of God. Did you know that? God wants you to have eternal life through Jesus and spend eternity with Him. Are you beginning to see the many ways in which we've been created in the likeness of God?

After God had created both men and women He told them to have children and to raise them and populate the earth. Isn't that amazing? Having children and raising them was God's idea. And in that way he allows us to participate with Him in raising future generations to love Him, serve Him and take charge of His creation. The fact that you've been placed in a family and you have parents to raise you means that you're a part of God's master plan too.

And do you know the most amazing thing of all? Verse 31 tells us that God looked over everything that He had created and considered it all. As He looked over the earth and the sky, the oceans and plants, the birds and the fish He decided it was all good and He was pleased with everything that His eye saw. But do you know what ELSE He looked at? The Bible says he looked over EVERYTHING that he had made — and that includes you! That's right. God looked at YOU long before you were ever born and He decided that YOU were good! He was pleased with you. Did you know that? God not only loves you — He LIKES you too! You please Him very much; you're the apple of His eye and you're a part of His creative plan.

Daily Study

Day 1

This is a special day! Man is about to appear on the scene. It's a special day because God is going to make humans, whom He will love and to whom He will entrust His beautiful creation. He is going to make them in the image of Himself.

Now, with your family, read today's passage Genesis 1:26-31. Think about these verses together. The Bible tells us that God chose to make man "in our image." It does not use the phrase "in my image."

In whose image were we made?

Who are the "we" suggested by the phrase "our"?

Day 2

Take a few minutes to read this week's Scripture verses. Encourage your children to quiet themselves and really think about the verses as you read them.

Now ask them:

What do you think it means when the Bible says we were to have dominion over the animals?

Does having dominion mean having any responsibilities, or is it just authority?

Does it surprise you that God would entrust the animals to our care?

Day 3

As always, quiet your busy minds and offer a simple prayer, asking the Lord to help you hear Him through His Word today. Now read the "Watering the Seedling" that goes with this week's lesson again.

Give each child a chance to answer today's question: *After God blessed his human creations he instructed them to "be fruitful and multiply." What does that tell us about God's thoughts on children and families?*

Day 4

Read this week's Scripture passage with your family one last time... slowly. Let the words sink in so that you actually *hear* them with your heart as well as your ears. Now ask each person present to pick a verse that they particularly noticed and share why that verse was meaningful to them. It's interesting how different verses strike different people at different times. You may be amazed at some of the things your children pull out of this passage.

The Fall

Genesis 3:1-7, 21

¹ Now the serpent was more crafty than any other beast of the field that the Lord God had made.

He said to the woman, "Did God actually say, 'You shall not eat of any tree in the garden'?" ² And the woman said to the serpent, "We may eat of the fruit of the trees in the garden' ³ but God said, 'You shall not eat of the fruit of the tree that is in the midst of the garden, neither shall you touch it, lest you die.'" ⁴ But the serpent said to the woman, "You will not surely die. ⁵ For God knows that when you eat of it your eyes will be opened, and you will be like God, knowing good and evil." ⁶ So when the woman saw that the tree was good for food, and that it was a delight to the eyes, and that the tree was to be desired to make one wise, she took of its fruit and ate, and she also gave some to her husband who was with her, and he ate. ⁷ Then the eyes of both were opened, and they knew that they were naked. And they sewed fig leaves together and made themselves loincloths.

²¹ And the Lord God made for Adam and for his wife garments of skins and clothed them.

The Seed

Our enemy tempts us to rebel against God by questioning His goodness.

 ## Planting the Seed

He said to the woman, "Did God actually say,"... Genesis 3:1a **ESV**

Additional Planting the Seed (Ages 11+)

[1] Now the serpent was more crafty than any other beast of the field that the Lord God had made.

He said to the woman, "Did God actually say, 'You shall not eat of any tree in the garden'?" Genesis 3:1 **ESV**

 ## Watering the Seedling

We learned in Genesis 1 that God created the Earth, the heavens, the oceans, plants, fish, birds and animals. He also created man and woman and asked them to take charge of the earth and His creation. He was pleased with all that He had created and said that it was all good. It's a beautiful story, isn't it?

But every story has a bad guy, doesn't it? Wherever there is good, there is also evil. Wherever there is a hero, there is also a villain. And in the story of God's creation things are no different.

The names of the first man and woman were Adam and Eve. They were living in a beautiful place. Can you imagine the perfect picnic? Can you imagine a place where the temperature is never too hot and never too cold? Can you imagine ants that look at your food but don't try to eat it or bite you? Can you imagine bees that drift past you buzzing happily but never stinging? Can you imagine every plant with perfect flowers, delicious smells and flawless leaves? God had placed Adam and Eve in just such a perfect place.

But God also gave them one rule. Just one. In Genesis chapter 2 He told them not to eat the fruit from one particular tree. Why did God tell them that? Because God was smarter than Adam and Eve and He knew that the fruit was bad for them in ways they couldn't understand. All they had to do was obey and everything would be fine.

And then the villain appears in our story. The Bible tells us that the serpent was the most crafty of all the animals. Do you know what "crafty" means? It means he was deceptive and tricky and that he could convince people into making bad choices.

And so the serpent began to ask questions. He asked Eve if she was sure about the directions God had given her. When she repeated what God had said, the serpent began to argue saying, "Surely that can't be right. God has lied to you. He wants to keep the best for Himself and prevent you from having what belongs to you!"

He persuaded both Eve and Adam that God had not dealt fairly with them — that God didn't have their best interests at heart. And so they deliberately disobeyed the one rule that God had given them. The Bible calls this 'sin'. When we disobey, we sin.

Do you remember what God told them would happen if they ate the fruit of that particular tree? He told them if they disobeyed, or sinned, they would die.

The Apostle James tells us in James 1:15, "Desire, when it has conceived, gives birth to sin, and sin when it is fully grown brings forth death."

That's what happened here, isn't it? Adam and Eve looked at the beautiful fruit of the forbidden tree and they desired it; they wanted to see what it tasted like and feel the juice of that fruit running down their chins. Their desire for that fruit became greater than their desire to obey God and became sin. And we know that sin brings death.

Did Adam and Eve fall over dead the moment they ate the fruit? No, they didn't, did they? But something terrible happened. Their life-connection to God died. They became cut off and alone for the first time. And they immediately realized that they had been tricked by the serpent and done evil.

Suddenly they began to experience shame and guilt for the first time. They tried to cover themselves and hide from God.

But even in their disobedience, God still loved them and verse 21 tells us that God clothed them with the skins of animals in order to hide their nakedness even though something awful had changed their relationship with God.

There is a pattern here that we need to understand. Whenever the villain in OUR story tries to tempt us and lead us toward evil, he still asks the same questions. He still asks us whether God REALLY said not to do something specific. And if we stand firm in speaking the truth about God, then the villain begins to question God's intentions. He tries to convince us that God is holding out on us, keeping the best for Himself and giving us second best.

Those ought to be warning signs. When we begin to question God and His kindness and goodness, we're in danger of sinning and harming our relationship with God, our life-connection.

Adam and Eve learned a painful truth, didn't they? And in questioning God they became the first human beings to rebel against the One who created them and gave them life. Adam and Eve may have been first to rebel, but they weren't the last. It's a pattern we'll see again and again as we study the Bible.

 ## Daily Study

Day 1

Read today's Scripture passage Genesis 3:1-7, 21. The Bible says that a serpent approached Eve in the garden.

Ask your children:

Who do you think the serpent really was?

Why do you think that? Although the Bible doesn't tell us the exact answer to that question, many people have assumed that the serpent was actually the devil, tempting Eve.

Do you believe that?

Day 2

This is a great opportunity to learn more about the ways in which the Enemy operates. Re-read the "Watering the Seedling" narrative. What was the very first question the serpent asked? Ask your children why they think he asked that question.

Now here's one of those questions that can lead to some great family discussions. Quiet everyone down and then give each child the opportunity to answer this question:

Does he still ask us, "Did God really say..." today?

Day 3

We've been learning all week about the way in which the serpent deceived Eve. If you think it would be helpful, take a moment to re-read this week's Scripture verses with your family. Eve responded to the serpent's question by repeating what God had said. THEN what did the serpent do? (Note: The serpent contradicted God, telling Eve that God was wrong.) Does the Enemy still do that today?

Can you share a time when the Enemy lied to you and told you that God was wrong about something? This is a great time for parents to share from their real life experience and let children ask questions about how you responded — or perhaps how you WISH you had responded!

Day 4

Go back and re-read this week's Scriptures or the "Watering the Seedling" narrative one last time. Gather your children and quiet your hearts to hear the Lord. After Adam and Eve ate the forbidden fruit they saw that they were naked and the Bible tells us in verse 21 that God clothed them using the skins of animals.

Ask your children this question:

Why they think the animals first died in the Bible? (Hint: After the people rebelled and sinned against God, innocent blood had to be shed.) Much later in the Bible we'll see that Jesus' blood was shed for the forgiveness of our sins.

Center a family discussion time around this question: *Do you see a pattern in the way sin must be dealt with?*

Noah and the Flood

Genesis 6:5-22

⁵ The Lord saw that the wickedness of man was great in the earth, and that every intention of the thoughts of his heart was only evil continually. ⁶ And the Lord regretted that he had made man on the earth, and it grieved him to his heart. ⁷ So the Lord said, "I will blot out man whom I have created from the face of the land, man and animals and creeping things and birds of the heavens, for I am sorry that I have made them." ⁸ But Noah found favor in the eyes of the Lord. ⁹ These are the generations of Noah. Noah was a righteous man, blameless in his generation. Noah walked with God. ¹⁰ And Noah had three sons, Shem, Ham, and Japheth.

¹¹ Now the earth was corrupt in God's sight, and the earth was filled with violence. ¹² And God saw the earth, and behold, it was corrupt, for all flesh had corrupted their way on the earth. ¹³ And God said to Noah, "I have determined to make an end of all flesh, for the earth is filled with violence through them. Behold, I will destroy them with the earth. ¹⁴ Make yourself an ark of gopher wood. Make rooms in the ark, and cover it inside and out with pitch. ¹⁵ This is how you are to make it: the length of the ark 300 cubits, its breadth 50 cubits, and its height 30 cubits. ¹⁶ Make a roof for the ark, and finish it

to a cubit above, and set the door of the ark in its side. Make it with lower, second, and third decks. ¹⁷ For behold, I will bring a flood of waters upon the earth to destroy all flesh in which is the breath of life under heaven. Everything that is on the earth shall die. ¹⁸ But I will establish my covenant with you, and you shall come into the ark, you, your sons, your wife, and your sons' wives with you. ¹⁹ And of every living thing of all flesh, you shall bring two of every sort into the ark to keep them alive with you. They shall be male and female. ²⁰ Of the birds according to their kinds, and of the animals according to their kinds, of every creeping thing of the ground, according to its kind, two of every sort shall come in to you to keep them alive. ²¹ Also take with you every sort of food that is eaten, and store it up. It shall serve as food for you and for them." ²² Noah did this; he did all that God commanded him.

The Seed

God hates sin but extends grace to those who love Him.

Planting the Seed

The Lord saw that the wickedness of man was great in the earth... but Noah found favor in the eyes of the Lord. Genesis 6: 5a, 8 **ESV**

Additional Planting the Seed (Ages 11+)

So the Lord said, "I will blot out man whom I have created from the face of the land, man and animals and creeping things and birds of the heavens, for I am sorry that I have made them." But Noah found favor in the eyes of the Lord. Genesis 6:7-8 **ESV**

Watering the Seedling

We learned that Adam and Eve were the first people to disobey God and sin, didn't we? I told you that there were many others who have followed in their footsteps.

In fact, the Bible tells us that so many people began doubting God's goodness and choosing their own desires instead of God's desires that God became weary of all that He had created.

In Genesis 6 we learn that men and women everywhere were constantly choosing to disobey God. They made evil choices all day every day. All they thought about was doing evil and disobeying God and it broke God's heart. He was so grieved at all the evil in the world that He made a painful choice. God decided to simply wipe out all mankind and start over from scratch.

Have you ever been working on a drawing or painting and things begin to go wrong? Pretty soon the flowers don't look like flowers and the clown looks like a monkey and nothing is turning out the way you planned it when you began. So what do you do? Sometimes you simply throw your painting away and get out a clean sheet of paper and start over. That's what God decided to do. His whole, beautiful creation was not turning out right and He decided to start over from the beginning.

But there was one man who was different — Noah. God liked Noah and saw that he was a good man, an honest man who loved God's rules and made good choices. God chose to make a special plan just for Noah and his family.

So God let Noah in on His plan. He took Noah aside and said to him, "That's it! I've had it, Noah! I'm going to make a fresh start. The world is filled with evil-doers and I'm going to destroy it all and begin again. But I want you to save just enough of my creation to start over again. You and your family and two of all the animals, birds and reptiles will begin the world again when I'm finished."

God went on to give Noah blueprints on how to build a boat. He told Noah all the dimensions and measurements and told him how many decks to build on the boat. He told him what sort of wood to use and how to seal the joints of the boat so that it wouldn't sink. He even told Noah where to put the window and door. And Noah obeyed God's every command, building the boat exactly the way God told him to build it.

Then, God did just as he had said: He brought a mighty flood that covered all the earth and only Noah, his family and the animals he had gathered survived to begin the world once more.

Did you know that when we choose evil it breaks God's heart? And did you know that when we choose to do the right thing and obey God's commandments, He notices? He's watching us, just the way He was watching Noah and it delights Him when we honor His ways and obey His rules.

And do you know what's really amazing? Even if those around us are making lots of bad choices, God will help those who love Him just like Noah and his family.

Daily Study

Day 1

Take a few minutes to gather your family together and read this week's Scriptures aloud: Genesis 6:5-22. In verse 5 we read that both the thoughts and the actions of men everywhere were sinful.

At the end of verse 6 it says that when God saw this He was "grieved." Ask your children if they know what the word "grieved" means

Invite your children to take a moment and think about this question before sharing their answers in turn:

What do we know about how God feels when we sin?

Day 2

Briefly refresh your children's memory about this week's Bible story.

Ask them if they can think of a situation where God might be grieved. This could be in their own life, in the life of a friend, or in the news.

Why would God be grieved when people disobey? This is a chance to dig deeper if the moment seems good. It's these kinds of open-ended questions that often allow children to pull out deep fears or concerns and share them. Be prepared to spend additional time exploring this question in the safe, loving environment of "family."

Day 3

Re-read the "Watering the Seedling" from today's lesson, or invite your children to take turns reading the

27

lesson aloud. The Bible tells us that "Noah walked with God' and "found favor in God's sight."

Give each child a turn to answer the question:
What are some ways you might walk with God and find favor in His sight?

Day 4

This is your last opportunity to review this week's story. If you feel it would be beneficial, consider re-reading the verses or the narrative aloud as a family. Thank the Lord for the study and discussion you've enjoyed together this week.

See if one or more of your children can answer this question:

Because Noah loved God, how did God respond? Remind your children that we know that God hates evil and sin, but He cares for those who love Him. Ask each child in turn:

How does that make you feel?

The Tower of Babel

Genesis 11:1-9

¹ Now the whole earth had one language and the same words. ² And as people migrated from the east, they found a plain in the land of Shinar and settled there. ³ And they said to one another, "Come, let us make bricks, and burn them thoroughly." And they had brick for stone, and bitumen for mortar. ⁴ Then they said, "Come, let us build ourselves a city and a tower with its top in the heavens, and let us make a name for ourselves, lest we be dispersed over the face of the whole earth." ⁵ And the Lord came down to see the city and the tower, which the children of man had built. ⁶ And the Lord said, "Behold, they are one people, and they have all one language, and this is only the beginning of what they will do. And nothing that they propose to do will now be impossible for them. ⁷ Come, let us go down and there confuse their language, so that they may not understand one another's speech." ⁸ So the Lord dispersed them from there over the face of all the earth, and they left off building the city. ⁹ Therefore its name was called Babel, because there the Lord confused the language of all the earth. And from there the Lord dispersed them over the face of all the earth.

The Seed

Men are proud and want to be in charge instead of obeying God.

 ## Planting the Seed

Pride goes before destruction,
and a haughty spirit before a fall. Proverbs 16:18 **ESV**

Additional Planting the Seed (Ages 11+)

So the Lord dispersed them from there over the face of all the earth, and they left off building the city. Genesis 11:8 **ESV**

 ## Watering the Seedling

Noah and his family begin to populate the earth over again after the Flood. Many years went by and men once again began to decide they didn't need God.

God had given some very specific directions after the great Flood. He told Noah and his sons and their wives to "be fruitful, multiply and fill the earth." In other words, God wanted men to spread out over all the earth and manage God's creation the way He had originally intended. God hoped that men would go to all the various parts of the earth and enjoy a relationship with their Creator.

But that's not what happened, is it? Instead, the Bible says that all the men gathered together in one place and refused to fill the earth the way God intended. Not only did the people refuse to do what God had asked, but instead they began to develop a plan to band more closely together.

They decided to build a great city where they could all live together. They also decided to build a tall tower so that they might become famous. We still do that today, don't we? Perhaps you know about the Empire State Building in New York, or the Sears tower in Chicago. In 2010 the tallest building in the world was built in the United Arab Emirates in north Africa. Each one of those buildings was built so that men in those cities could claim, "We have the tallest building. Ours is best, ours is biggest!"

Men weren't so different in the Bible times, were they? They wanted to build the tallest tower in the world to show how special they were. But more importantly they wanted to build a great city where all the people could be together and pat themselves on the back for all they had accomplished. They were filled with pride and they wanted to worship themselves instead of worshipping God. Once again men were deliberately disobeying God's instruction, and once again God wasn't happy with what was happening.

After the Flood, God had promised that He would never again send another flood to wipe out the earth and He kept His word. Instead of destroying the wicked people, He chose to spoil their plan.

The people of Babel were going about their business when, suddenly, something miraculous happened. All the people began to speak in different languages! No one could understand what others were saying. They stared at each other, wide-eyed and confused. What had happened? Why couldn't they understand each other? What had caused this strange thing to happen?

God watched as they became more and more

frustrated, unable to communicate or to understand each other. Surely God was pleased when they gave up building their great city and tall tower and scattered over all the earth. That's what God had asked them to do in the first place, isn't it? They chose not to obey so God confused them. When they could no longer talk and make plans together, they wandered away and went to many different lands.

How often do we decide to ignore God's instructions and try to do things our own way? How often do we try to show off and make everyone else think that we're the biggest, the best, the smartest or the most beautiful? How often are we tempted to believe that we don't really need God at all? Pride is a powerful force that deceives us and tells us that we're more important than even God.

It's really kind of silly, isn't it? The Lord God made us all and gave us whatever skills and resources we have. So it's really all about Him, isn't it? It was never about us the way the foolish people of Babel thought. In Proverbs 16:18 the Bible tells us that "Pride goes before destruction, and a haughty spirit before a fall."

Do you know what a haughty spirit is? It means looking down on others and believing you're better than they are. In this case, the foolish people of Babel were so filled with pride that they even looked down on their Creator, believing that they were better than God Himself. But after God confused their language, their plans were destroyed and they fell away one by one just the way Proverbs said.

Isn't it interesting that God has many ways of confronting our pride? Wouldn't it have been easier for the people of Babel if they had just done what God asked them to do in the first place and scattered out over all the earth? Worshipping God and following His plan is always better than trying to do things our own way as the confused people of Babel found out.

 ## Daily Study

Day 1

Read this week's Scripture passage aloud: Genesis 11:1-9. Or consider allowing each child to read one verse, passing the Bible around as you share the reading task. Now draw everyone's attention to verse 4 where the people said, "... let us make a name for ourselves." See if any of your children can tell what the people meant by this statement. One or more of your children might use the word "pride." Remind your children that there are two kinds of "pride." See if your children can describe them both. (Note: there's the good, positive kind of pride we feel when we do something good or right or courageous. But there is also the kind of pride born of arrogance, of thinking better of ourselves than we deserve.)

Day 2

Gather your children together and quiet your hearts before the Lord. Pray and ask the Lord to help you understand His Word today as you study it together. Remind the children about this week's passage, or invite one of them to re-read the text from Genesis 11.

Invite each child to share their thoughts on these questions:

After God confused their language and none of them could understand one another, how do you think they felt?

Were they still proud?

What does the word 'humble' mean?

Day 3

James 4:6 tells us that "God opposes the proud, but gives grace to the humble." Can you put that verse into your own words and share how you might use that verse in your own life?

One by one, ask each child to think of an example where they've seen God 'oppose the proud' or 'give grace to the humble.' This is a great question to turn into prayer, seeking forgiveness for times we've been proud, or thanking God for times he has given us grace in our humility.

Day 4

Verse 9 tells us that God dispersed the people over all the earth, speaking many different languages. Discuss with your family:

Have you ever wondered why people in every country speak a different language?

Did you know that there are men and women whose job is to translate the Bible into every one of those languages so that everyone can read God's word for themselves?

Have you begun to make a habit of reading God's word every day yourself?

Share when and where you like to read the Bible (or have the Bible read to you.)

The Call of Abram

Genesis 12:1-7

[1] Now the Lord said to Abram, "Go from your country and your kindred and your father's house to the land that I will show you. [2] And I will make of you a great nation, and I will bless you and make your name great, so that you will be a blessing. [3] I will bless those who bless you, and him who dishonors you I will curse, and in you all the families of the earth shall be blessed."

[4] So Abram went, as the Lord had told him, and Lot went with him. Abram was seventy-five years old when he departed from Haran. [5] And Abram took Sarai his wife, and Lot his brother's son, and all their possessions that they had gathered, and the people that they had acquired in Haran, and they set out to go to the land of Canaan. When they came to the land of Canaan, [6] Abram passed through the land to the place at Shechem, to the oak of Moreh. At that time the Canaanites were in the land. [7] Then the Lord appeared to Abram and said, "To your offspring I will give this land." So he built there an altar to the Lord, who had appeared to him.

The Seed

God establishes a family of His own.

Planting the Seed

Now the Lord said to Abram... I will make of you a great nation, and I will bless you.
Genesis 12:1a, 2a **ESV**

Additional Planting the Seed (Ages 11+)

And I will make of you a great nation, and I will bless you and make your name great, so that you will be a blessing. ³ I will bless those who bless you, and him who dishonors you I will curse, and in you all the families of the earth shall be blessed.
Genesis 12:2-3 **ESV**

Watering the Seedling

In Genesis 1 we learned that God created man in his own image. Among many things, that means God created us to be relational. We like to be with other people — loving and serving and building relationships. That makes sense because God the Father, Jesus the Son and the Holy Spirit had been enjoying fellowship since before the beginning of time. Wouldn't it be reasonable to assume that if God created us in His likeness, we would be relational too?

We can try to live our lives alone, but in the end that's not how we were created. We were created to enjoy relationships with God and with other people.

But we've seen how men chose time after time to ignore God and to break fellowship with Him by making selfish, prideful choices. God destroyed the evil men in the Flood and then he scattered the evil people of the world at Babel. But God still longed for fellowship with His creation; He wanted to have a relationship with men and women. He wanted a family of His own — a family that loved Him for who He was and ultimately a family that would give birth to Jesus, the Messiah.

So God began writing a new chapter in His great history book. God found a man named Abram who had a wife Sarai and a nephew named Lot. Now you might ask, "Why did God choose Abram instead of some other man?" I'm not sure, but God knew what He was doing and Abram turned out to be a man who loved God and obeyed Him, even when it was very hard to do so.

God gave Abram some very specific instructions. We've seen that before, haven't we? God gave Adam and Eve very specific instructions. He'll tell us what He wants us to do; we just need to learn to listen.

Well, Abram listened. And what's more, Abram OBEYED! Verse 4 of Genesis 12 tells us this, "So Abram went, as the Lord had told him"

So often in our studies we've seen men who did NOT do what the Lord told them to do. They did NOT go where God told them to go. But not Abram! No sir! Abram was a wise man and he loved God. He did exactly what God told him to do and he went exactly where God told him to go.

God directed Abram to the land of Canaan. Even though there were already people living in Canaan, God promised Abram that this land would be his.

And do you know what Abram did? He didn't ask God how that could happen. He didn't ask God to make the Canaanites go away. He didn't argue with God that there were many Canaanites and not so many of them. Nope.

Instead he thanked God for the land he had been promised. The Bible says that Abram built an altar right there on that spot and Abram gave thanks. Abram must have offered sacrifices on the altar and as far as the Bible tells us, Abram never doubted God's promise.

Has God made promises to you? Of course He has! Hebrews 13:5 says this, "I will never leave you nor forsake you." (ESV) In Jeremiah 29:11 God makes this promise: "For I know the plans I have for you, declares the Lord, plans for welfare and not for evil, to give you a future and a hope." (ESV)

God has given you MANY promises even though you're still young. Perhaps you'd like to respond to those promises the same way Abram reacted, by thanking God for His goodness and faithfulness.

Did you see the special promise that God gave Abram right in the middle of our passage? In verse 3 God says, "in you all the families of the earth shall be blessed." What do you suppose God was talking about there? I think God was talking about Jesus in that passage. He was telling Abram a secret: someday a Savior would be born through Abram's ancestors and that the this Savior would be a blessing to all the earth.

Do you think Abram understood all of that? I'll bet he didn't. I'll bet it was all confusing to Abram. But he thanked God anyway. He thanked Him for the parts he DID understand and he thanked Him for the parts he didn't understand.

God had found a man He could trust; a man who loved God and obeyed Him. I want to be that kind of person, don't you?

Daily Study

Day 1

It's always good to pray together before you begin each day's discussion. Quiet your heart and ask the Lord to speak to you as you read His Word. Read this week's verses: Genesis 12:1-7. God decided that he wanted a family of his own and so he began by selecting a man who loved him. Through Abram, God planned to build a great family.

Here's a good question for discussion:

What is the first thing God asks Abram to do in verse 1?

Day 2

Read this week's verses once more: Genesis 12:1-7. In verses 2 and 3, God makes Abram a promise. Do you see it? Let each child and parent retell the promise in their own words. You may be surprised at the various ways that others describe God's promise. You might even choose to write down the key words and phrases that come up as you discuss these verses.

Day 3

Read this week's "Watering the Seedling" from your *Firmly Planted* manual aloud or take turns reading it as you pass the book around the table. Check out verse 4 and ask these questions:

What does Abram do in response to God's orders?

Do you think it pleases God when we obey Him? Can you share some ways that you've obeyed God this week?

Encourage each child to think back over this past week and see if they can think of specific ways they've obeyed God this week.

Day 4

Read this week's Scriptures one last time: Genesis 12:1-7. Thank the Lord for all you've learned together this week as a family. In verse 7 we learn that after God made a promise to Abram, he built an altar there. An altar is a place of thanksgiving. Abram thanked God for all he had done for him. Ask your kids:

Can you share a time when you thanked God for something He did for you?

Let each member take as much time as needed to talk about things that they've been thankful for.

Isaac on the Altar

Genesis 22:1-19

¹ After these things God tested Abraham and said to him, "Abraham!" And he said, "Here I am." ² He said, "Take your son, your only son Isaac, whom you love, and go to the land of Moriah, and offer him there as a burnt offering on one of the mountains of which I shall tell you." ³ So Abraham rose early in the morning, saddled his donkey, and took two of his young men with him, and his son Isaac. And he cut the wood for the burnt offering and arose and went to the place of which God had told him. ⁴ On the third day Abraham lifted up his eyes and saw the place from afar. ⁵ Then Abraham said to his young men, "Stay here with the donkey; I and the boy will go over there and worship and come again to you." ⁶ And Abraham took the wood of the burnt offering and laid it on Isaac his son. And he took in his hand the fire and the knife. So they went both of them together. ⁷ And Isaac said to his father Abraham, "My father!" And he said, "Here I am, my son." He said, "Behold, the fire and the wood, but where is the lamb for a burnt offering?"⁸ Abraham said, "God will provide for himself the lamb for a burnt offering, my son." So they went both of them together.

⁹ When they came to the place of which God had told him, Abraham built the altar there and

laid the wood in order and bound Isaac his son and laid him on the altar, on top of the wood. [10] Then Abraham reached out his hand and took the knife to slaughter his son. [11] But the angel of the Lord called to him from heaven and said, "Abraham, Abraham!" And he said, "Here I am." [12] He said, "Do not lay your hand on the boy or do anything to him, for now I know that you fear God, seeing you have not withheld your son, your only son, from me." [13] And Abraham lifted up his eyes and looked, and behold, behind him was a ram, caught in a thicket by his horns. And Abraham went and took the ram and offered it up as a burnt offering instead of his son. [14] So Abraham called the name of that place, "The Lord will provide"; as it is said to this day, "On the mount of the Lord it shall be provided."

[15] And the angel of the Lord called to Abraham a second time from heaven [16] and said, "By myself I have sworn, declares the Lord, because you have done this and have not withheld your son, your only son, [17] I will surely bless you, and I will surely multiply your offspring as the stars of heaven and as the sand that is on the seashore. And your offspring shall possess the gate of his enemies, [18] and in your offspring shall all the nations of the earth be blessed, because you have obeyed my voice." [19] So Abraham returned to his young men, and they arose and went together to Beersheba. And Abraham lived at Beersheba.

 ## The Seed

God tests Abraham's faith by asking him to sacrifice his only son Isaac.

Planting the Seed

Abraham said, "God will provide for himself the lamb for a burnt offering, my son."
Genesis 22:8a **ESV**

Additional Planting the Seed
(Ages 11+)

So Abraham called the name of that place, "The Lord will provide"; as it is said to this day, "On the mount of the Lord it shall be provided."
Genesis 22:14 **ESV**

Watering the Seedling

We learned that God chose a man named Abram to establish his own family, and we learned that Abram was a man who obeyed God even when it was hard.

As God and Abram became friends, God offered Abram a deal, telling him that if he would obey God and be blameless, then God would give Abram many children. Then God's blessing would be on Abram's family forever.

As part of that agreement God changed Abram's name to Abraham. God often changed people's names in the Bible to signify a new beginning. Jacob became Israel; Jesus changed Simon's name to Peter. So Abram had become Abraham and now he had a son named Isaac. Abraham loved Isaac very, very much. Isaac meant more to Abraham than anything else on earth, except for Abraham's love for God.

One day God told Abraham to take his son Isaac and go to a particular mountain to offer Isaac as a sacrifice there. Of course Abraham was very upset and afraid, but he obeyed. He gathered two of his servants, his donkey and wood to build a fire and set off with his son Isaac.

After several days they arrived at the mountain and Abraham and Isaac went alone the rest of the way. Isaac carried the wood for the burnt offering and Abraham took only his knife and a flint to light a fire.

Suddenly Isaac looked around and realized they had no lamb for their offering and he asked his father where they might find a sheep. But Abraham answered saying, "God will provide a lamb for us," and they continued their journey.

At last they arrived at the place God had instructed them to go and Abraham began piling up the wood to build a fire. Now all this time Abraham knew that God had asked him to sacrifice his son, Isaac. Can you imagine how sad Abraham must have been as they walked for three days toward that mountain? What do you think Abraham was thinking?

When Abraham told Isaac that God would provide a lamb for them, do you think he was just telling a white lie so that Isaac wouldn't be worried? Or do you think Abraham really believed what he said?

Abraham must have believed his own words, and I'm sure he hoped and prayed as they walked toward Mount Moriah together. But in the end, Abraham was going to hold up his end of his covenant with God and obey the Lord, no matter how hard it was.

So Abraham had Isaac lie down on top of the wood pile on the altar. Now that the time for the sacrifice had come, and God had still not provided a lamb, Abraham obediently took out his knife and prepared to offer his son Isaac. But at the last minute, God suddenly spoke, telling Abraham NOT to harm Isaac. Then provided a ram for the sacrifice.

Can you imagine how relieved and thankful Abraham was at that moment? He had trusted God and obeyed... and the Lord did not let him down. God came through for Abraham at the last moment.

And because Abraham had obeyed, God reaffirmed his covenant with Abraham; he would have many, many descendants, they would possess Canaan, and all the nations of the world would be blessed through Abraham's descendants.

Do you know who one of those descendants was? Through Abraham, and through his son Isaac, God gave us Jesus the Messiah! God was faithful and true to his word.

Just as God the father would someday offer His only Son Jesus as a sacrifice for our sins, so too Abraham had been willing to offer his son Isaac as a sacrifice.

Abraham obeyed God even when it was hard. And Abraham learned that God can always be trusted.

 ## Daily Study

Day 1

Quiet your hearts from the business of the day and then read this week's Scripture passage aloud: Genesis 22:1-19. Verse 1 tells us that God tested Abraham. Get everyone's attention and use these questions for discussion:

Did you know that God sometimes tests people?

Can you think of any ways he might test you?

Has there ever been a time when you knew you were being tested?

Today's questions can be a rich time of discussion. Don't be in a rush to 'get through' the assignment. Let each member of the family contemplate and share.

Day 2

Read aloud this week's "Watering the Seedling" from your *Firmly Planted* manual. In verse 2, God tells Abraham, "Take your son, your only son." John 3:16 tells us that God gave his "only son" for our sins. Here are some questions that might spark some discussion:

Who was the only son that God gave?

Can you see how the story of Abraham and Isaac is similar to the story of God the Father and Jesus?

How are the stories similar?

How are they different?

You may need to help younger children see the similarities and differences as you talk through this important Old Testament image of God's provision for sin.

Day 3

In verse 8 Abraham tells Isaac, "God will provide for himself the lamb." In John 1:29 John the Baptist sees Jesus approaching and says, "Behold, the Lamb of God, who takes away the sin of the world!" In Genesis, God provided a real lamb. Today's discussion follows up on yesterday's questions.

Who is the Lamb of God that has been provided to take away our sins?

Pray and thank God for providing the "Lamb of God" to take away our sins.

Day 4

In John 1:12 we read about Jesus, the Lamb of God. "But to all who receive [Jesus], those who believed in his name, he gave the right to become children of God."

Have you told Jesus, the lamb of God, that you believe in him and want him to take away your sins?

Parents, ask your kids to share when that happened to them. If they have never done that, you might ask them if they would like to do that today! Gently instruct your kids how to ask Jesus to be their Savior and Lord.

Parents, this may be a profoundly important day in the spiritual growth of your child. Take as long as necessary to give each child a chance to confess their need of a savior and ask Jesus to come into their life and take away their sins.

Jacob, Rachel and Leah

Genesis 29

¹ Then Jacob went on his journey and came to the land of the people of the east. ² As he looked, he saw a well in the field, and behold, three flocks of sheep lying beside it, for out of that well the flocks were watered. The stone on the well's mouth was large, ³ and when all the flocks were gathered there, the shepherds would roll the stone from the mouth of the well and water the sheep, and put the stone back in its place over the mouth of the well.

⁴ Jacob said to them, "My brothers, where do you come from?" They said, "We are from Haran." ⁵ He said to them, "Do you know Laban the son of Nahor?" They said, "We know him." ⁶ He said to them, "Is it well with him?" They said, "It is well; and see, Rachel his daughter is coming with the sheep!" ⁷ He said, "Behold, it is still high day; it is not time for the livestock to be gathered together. Water the sheep and go, pasture them." ⁸ But they said, "We cannot until all the flocks are gathered together and the stone is rolled from the mouth of the well; then we water the sheep."

⁹ While he was still speaking with them, Rachel came with her father's sheep, for she was a shepherdess. ¹⁰ Now as soon as Jacob saw Rachel the daughter of Laban his mother's brother, and the sheep of Laban his mother's brother,

Jacob came near and rolled the stone from the well's mouth and watered the flock of Laban his mother's brother.[11] Then Jacob kissed Rachel and wept aloud. [12] And Jacob told Rachel that he was her father's kinsman, and that he was Rebekah's son, and she ran and told her father.

[13] As soon as Laban heard the news about Jacob, his sister's son, he ran to meet him and embraced him and kissed him and brought him to his house. Jacob told Laban all these things, [14] and Laban said to him, "Surely you are my bone and my flesh!" And he stayed with him a month.

[15] Then Laban said to Jacob, "Because you are my kinsman, should you therefore serve me for nothing? Tell me, what shall your wages be?" [16] Now Laban had two daughters. The name of the older was Leah, and the name of the younger was Rachel. [17] Leah's eyes were weak, but Rachel was beautiful in form and appearance. [18] Jacob loved Rachel. And he said, "I will serve you seven years for your younger daughter Rachel." [19] Laban said, "It is better that I give her to you than that I should give her to any other man; stay with me." [20] So Jacob served seven years for Rachel, and they seemed to him but a few days because of the love he had for her.

[21] Then Jacob said to Laban, "Give me my wife that I may go in to her, for my time is completed." [22] So Laban gathered together all the people of the place and made a feast. [23] But in the evening he took his daughter Leah and brought her to Jacob, and he went in to her. [24] (Laban gave his female servant Zilpah to his daughter Leah to be her servant.)[25] And in the morning, behold, it was Leah! And Jacob said to Laban, "What is this you have done to me? Did I not serve with you for Rachel? Why then have you deceived me?" [26]

49

Laban said, "It is not so done in our country, to give the younger before the firstborn. ²⁷ Complete the week of this one, and we will give you the other also in return for serving me another seven years." ²⁸ Jacob did so, and completed her week. Then Laban gave him his daughter Rachel to be his wife. ²⁹ (Laban gave his female servant Bilhah to his daughter Rachel to be her servant.) ³⁰ So Jacob went in to Rachel also, and he loved Rachel more than Leah, and served Laban for another seven years.

³¹ When the Lord saw that Leah was hated, he opened her womb, but Rachel was barren. ³² And Leah conceived and bore a son, and she called his name Reuben, for she said, "Because the Lord has looked upon my affliction; for now my husband will love me." ³³ She conceived again and bore a son, and said, "Because the Lord has heard that I am hated, he has given me this son also." And she called his name Simeon. ³⁴ Again she conceived and bore a son, and said, "Now this time my husband will be attached to me, because I have borne him three sons." Therefore his name was called Levi. ³⁵ And she conceived again and bore a son, and said, "This time I will praise the Lord." Therefore she called his name Judah. Then she ceased bearing.

The Seed

God gives a special blessing to those who are not loved.

Planting the Seed

"When the Lord saw that Leah was hated, he opened her womb..." Genesis 29:31a **ESV**

Additional Planting the Seed
(Ages 11+)

And she conceived again and bore a son, and said, "This time I will praise the Lord." Therefore she called his name Judah. Genesis 29:35a **ESV**

Watering the Seedling

God spared Isaac by providing a ram for Abraham's sacrifice, so Isaac grew and had a family of his own. One of Isaac's sons was a man named Jacob.

One day Isaac sent Jacob to go and visit his uncle Laban in search of a suitable wife. When Jacob arrived in the land of Laban he stopped at a well where shepherds were waiting to water their sheep. Jacob was asking about Laban when suddenly Laban's beautiful daughter Rachel came toward the well with her sheep.

Now the shepherds who were gathered around the well were waiting for all the other shepherds to arrive because there was a huge stone that covered the well. The stone was so heavy that all of the shepherds together had a difficult time rolling it aside.

Do you ever 'show off' when you're trying to impress someone? Well that's exactly what Jacob did! He took one look at his beautiful cousin Rachel and he immediately fell head-over-heels in love. Jacob made sure that Rachel was watching and then walked over and moved the enormous stone all by himself! Rachel was surely impressed with Jacob's great strength, and that's just what Jacob wanted.

Jacob watered all of Rachel's sheep for her while she watched this powerful stranger. When he was finished, Jacob couldn't help himself; he kissed Rachel. He was so happy to have found his wife that he broke into tears!

Jacob explained that he was her cousin. Rachel went and told her father Laban that his nephew was at the well. Laban ran out to greet Jacob and welcomed him into his home where Jacob stayed for a month as a guest.

But Jacob was intent on making Rachel his wife and so he struck an agreement with his uncle Laban. Jacob would work for Laban for seven years. At the end of that time, Laban would give Rachel to Jacob as his wife.

The years went quickly and Jacob's wedding day finally arrived. But when Jacob woke up after his wedding night he made a shocking discovery. Laban had tricked him and sent him Rachel's older sister Leah to be his wife. In the darkness, Jacob didn't realize he had been tricked. Jacob was very upset because Leah was nothing like her beautiful sister; Jacob didn't think Leah was beautiful at all. The really sad thing was that Leah knew that Jacob had been deceived into marrying her. She knew that Jacob didn't love her the way he loved Rachel.

Jacob complained to Laban and Laban explained that in their country a younger sister couldn't marry until after her older sister had married. So he made Jacob another offer: In a week he would be allowed to marry Rachel as well, but Jacob would have to work for another seven years. So the agreement was made.

Jacob spent seven more years working for his uncle Laban and during that time he was thrilled to have his beautiful wife Rachel. But he was never even slightly happy to have her older sister Leah as a wife too. He didn't love Leah at all and Leah was very sad.

But God saw Leah's heart and God did something extraordinary: He gave Leah four sons! Rachel was unable to have children, but Leah gave her husband Jacob four beautiful boys: Reuben, Simeon, Levi and Judah. And Leah was certain each time that Jacob would love her for giving him a son. But Jacob still only loved Rachel.

When her fourth son was born, Leah chose a very special name for him. She named him Judah, which means "Praise God!" Leah must have realized that Jacob would always be in love with her beautiful, younger sister. So Leah chose to praise God even though her life was very hard and unhappy.

Because Leah was unloved, God chose to bless her in a very special way. Do you know what happened? It was through that fourth son Judah that God chose to bring Jesus the Messiah into the world. In Revelation 5:5 we read these words describing Jesus: "Then one of the elders said to me, 'Do not weep! See, the Lion of the tribe of Judah, the Root of David, has triumphed.'"

That's right. God chose poor, lonely Leah to be a part of Jesus' family tree. Jesus was born through the bloodline of Leah's fourth son Judah, and through King David who was still ten generations in the future. God had a plan from the very beginning of time for Jesus's birth and He chose each of Jesus' ancestors with care. God heard Leah's cry and blessed her through her children's children.

Daily Study

Day 1

Find a quiet place to gather your family together and read this week's Scripture aloud: Genesis 29. In verse 16 we read, "Now Laban had two daughters. The name of the older was Leah, and the name of the younger was Rachel. Leah's eyes were weak, but Rachel was beautiful in form and appearance."

If Rachel was "beautiful in form and appearance" what does that imply about Leah?

What do you think Leah looked like?

Day 2

Yesterday we talked about Rachel and Leah's appearance. We all look different. Pray with your children before you begin and ask the Lord to open their eyes and help them see God's truth in this week's story. Perhaps you have a sibling, neighbor or friend who you think is more beautiful or more handsome than you are.

How do you think Leah felt, compared to her sister Rachel?

Let each person at the table answer. You might want to make a list of each answer on paper or a whiteboard and talk about them.

Day 3

Read this week's "Watering the Seed" section from your *Firmly Planted* book aloud, or let everyone at the table take turns reading a paragraph. It was the custom in Jacob's day for the older daughter to marry before the younger daughter. But apparently nobody had ever asked to marry Leah. Why do you think that might be?

Start a discussion on this topic by using these questions:

Can you tell about a time when you didn't get picked for a team or activity, or when you didn't get invited to a party or event?

How did that make you feel?

Invite each person at the table to share their own story. Almost all of us have felt unchosen or left out at one time or another. It's important for us to realize God sees our disappointment, and God loves us all the same.

Day 4

Review all that you've talked about this week as a family. Now read Genesis 29 one final time. Concentrate on verse 31 which tells us that "Leah was hated". Apparently Jacob loved the beautiful Rachel more than he loved Leah. Maybe he even hated her. But God blessed Leah with children because God has no favorites. How does that make you feel? The point, of course, is for each child (and parent!) to grasp that profound truth. God loves me no matter what anyone else feels about me. The Lord hears my cries and will bless me.

God Wrestles with Jacob

Genesis 32:22-32

22 The same night he arose and took his two wives, his two female servants, and his eleven children, and crossed the ford of the Jabbok. 23 He took them and sent them across the stream, and everything else that he had. 24 And Jacob was left alone. And a man wrestled with him until the breaking of the day. 25 When the man saw that he did not prevail against Jacob, he touched his hip socket, and Jacob's hip was put out of joint as he wrestled with him. 26 Then he said, "Let me go, for the day has broken." But Jacob said, "I will not let you go unless you bless me." 27 And he said to him, "What is your name?" And he said, "Jacob." 28 Then he said, "Your name shall no longer be called Jacob, but Israel, for you have striven with God and with men, and have prevailed." 29 Then Jacob asked him, "Please tell me your name." But he said, "Why is it that you ask my name?" And there he blessed him. 30 So Jacob called the name of the place Peniel, saying, "For I have seen God face to face, and yet my life has been delivered." 31 The sun rose upon him as he passed Penuel, limping because of his hip. 32 Therefore to this day the people of Israel do not eat the sinew of the thigh that is on the hip socket, because he touched the socket of Jacob's hip on the sinew of the thigh.

The Seed

God wrestles with Jacob and blesses him at Peniel.

 ## Planting the Seed

"Your name shall no longer be called Jacob, but Israel..." Genesis 32:28a **ESV**

Additional Planting the Seed (Ages 11+)

Then he said, "Your name shall no longer be called Jacob, but Israel, for you have striven with God and with men, and have prevailed."
Genesis 32:22 **ESV**

 ## Watering the Seedling

Do you remember that God changed Abram's name to Abraham? Today we're going to learn about another man who had his name changed by God.

This is the story of Abraham's grandson Jacob. Jacob had lied to his father Isaac and stolen his twin brother Esau's blessing. Jacob knew that Esau had every right to be angry with him and now Esau was coming after Jacob with 400 men and Jacob was very frightened. He sent his family ahead to cross a river and get safely away from Esau, but Jacob stayed behind. Jacob sent many valuable gifts to Esau, hoping he wouldn't be angry but inside Jacob was terrified.

Jacob began praying, reminding God of the many promises to his grandfather Abraham and that God promised to protect and bless Abraham's descendants.

So here was Abraham's grandson Jacob, alone and frightened late at night.

Suddenly Jacob found himself wrestling with a "man". They wrestled throughout the night until the sun finally came up but Jacob would not give up. Jacob was desperate.

Now it turns out that this was no mere man with whom Jacob was wrestling. This was actually God Himself. We know this because later in the story Jacob names the place where all this happened Peniel which means "I have seen God face to face!"

So Jacob spent the whole night wrestling with God Himself. We're not sure exactly what was being said during that fight. Perhaps Jacob continued to remind God of his promises to his grandfather Abraham and his father Isaac. Perhaps Jacob was asking forgiveness for having deceived his brother Esau too. The Bible doesn't tell us.

What it does tell us is that when morning came God blessed Jacob and changed his name from Jacob, which means "deceiver", to Israel, which means "he wrestles with God" or "God wrestles". Jacob had wrestled with God and from that day on he was a changed man. God had changed him both inside and out.

During their struggle Jacob's hip had been injured when God touched it and this changed man, Israel, always walked with a limp after that. Even today Jewish people don't eat thigh meat because they remember that Israel's thigh was injured the night he wrestled with God and God touched him.

And just in case you wondered, when Israel met with his twin brother Esau later that morning they had a wonderful reunion. It turned out that Esau wasn't angry after all and had long ago forgiven his brother for his deceitfulness.

Daily Study

Day 1

As always, gather your family together in a quiet place. Turn off the cell phone and the television and pray, asking the Lord to give you insights into His Word today. Now read this week's Scripture aloud: Genesis 32:22-32. Near the beginning of the text in Genesis 32:24 we read that Jacob wrestled with "a man." But later in verse 30 Jacob says, "I have seen God face to face."

Who was the "man" that wrestled with Jacob?

Encourage everyone to talk about the importance of this revelation: It wasn't just a man with whom Jacob was wrestling; it was God Himself.

Day 2

Read this week's "Watering the Seedling" narrative from your *Firmly Planted Family Study Guide*. Jacob tells God, "I will not let you go unless you bless me."

Do you think Jacob was wrong to say such a thing to God? In verse 29 we read, "and there he (God) blessed him (Jacob)."

How did God feel about Jacob's request?

Let your family talk through this question together. There may be disagreement whether it's right to speak to God in such a way. Draw their attention to verse 29 where we learn that apparently God didn't object to being challenged and in fact he complied with Jacob's request.

Day 3

Today's question offers each person a chance to think

beyond the obvious and it may take a few minutes for the ideas to begin to flow. Once the children "get" this concept you may be bombarded with lots and lots of ideas. Write them down on a piece of paper or whiteboard and talk about them.

Can you think of any ways that we wrestle with God today?

What about when we pray?

Are there any areas of your life where you need to wrestle with God for His blessing and provision?

Day 4

Read the narrative one last time and then ask the Lord to meet with you today and speak directly to each person in the room. Today's question is an open-ended one that may lead in some unexpected directions. Draw your children and perhaps set the tone by going first and sharing your own insight as you've been studying God's Word all week. Here's the question:

Was there anything in this week's lesson that God spoke to you about personally?

The Twelve Sons of Jacob

Genesis 35:22b-26

²²ᵇ Now the sons of Jacob were twelve. ²³ The sons of Leah: Reuben (Jacob's firstborn), Simeon, Levi, Judah, Issachar, and Zebulun. ²⁴ The sons of Rachel: Joseph and Benjamin. ²⁵ The sons of Bilhah, Rachel's servant: Dan and Naphtali.²⁶ The sons of Zilpah, Leah's servant: Gad and Asher. These were the sons of Jacob who were born to him in Paddan-aram.

²⁷ And Jacob came to his father Isaac at Mamre, or Kiriath-arba (that is, Hebron), where Abraham and Isaac had sojourned. ²⁸ Now the days of Isaac were 180 years. ²⁹ And Isaac breathed his last, and he died and was gathered to his people, old and full of days. And his sons Esau and Jacob buried him.

The Seed

God builds the nation of Israel through the twelve sons of Jacob.

Planting the Seed

Now the sons of Jacob were twelve.
Genesis 35:22b **ESV**

Additional Planting the Seed
(Ages 11+)

> The sons of Leah: Reuben (Jacob's firstborn), Simeon, Levi, Judah, Issachar, and Zebulun. [24] The sons of Rachel: Joseph and Benjamin. [25] The sons of Bilhah, Rachel's servant: Dan and Naphtali.[26] The sons of Zilpah, Leah's servant: Gad and Asher.
> Genesis 35:23-26 **ESV**

Watering the Seedling

Remember that God had promised Abraham in Genesis 12:2 that he would make Abraham's family into a great nation. God spoke again in Genesis 22:17, saying "I will surely bless you, and I will surely multiply your offspring as the stars of heaven and as the sand that is on the seashore." Through Jacob and his family, God is continuing the process of keeping that promise.

Jacob received his father's blessing and married Leah and Rachel. Both of Jacob's wives were given a servant to help in her new home. In those days men could have more than one wife so Jacob actually ended up with a total of four wives: Rachel and her servant Bilhah, and Leah and her servant Zilpah. Families were quite different then, weren't they?

In the course of time, Jacob (now called Israel after God wrestled with him and changed his name) finds himself with a total of twelve sons by his four wives. These twelve sons become the building blocks on which God raises the twelve tribes (or families) of the nation of Israel. Remember when God started to establish a family of his own through Abraham back in Genesis 12? Now we see God's plan beginning to take shape. Out of these twelve tribes will come the millions of blood-related ancestors that would become God's chosen people, the nation of Israel.

Also, remember that God had said over and over again that the descendants of Abraham, Isaac and Jacob would be a blessing to all the peoples of the world. This is the most exciting and important part in this entire story. As God steadily weaves his tapestry of grace, there is a beautiful thread woven throughout all these names and men, tribes and generations. That thread would someday link Abraham, Isaac and Jacob to Jesus, the Messiah. It would eventually bring millions of additional ancestors into the family of God — people who were not blood-related to Jacob, but who would be adopted as sons and daughters through Jesus, the Messiah. This is how Jacob and his 12 sons would be a blessing to all nations.

The Bible is filled with the stories of these twelve tribes and their adventures — both good and bad. We'll learn more about them in the months ahead. Right now it may all seem a little confusing, but remember: it was never confusing to God. Like a Grand Master chess champion, he was planning his strategy far in advance. He was looking more than 40 generations into the future, fulfilling His promise to build the nation of Israel and provide a way for you and me to become a part of God's own family through Jesus Christ.

Daily Study

Day 1

Read this week's Scripture aloud: Genesis 35:22b-26. Invite the Holy Spirit to move among your family this week and give each member insight.

From Abram, God brought forth a son Isaac. And to Isaac was born Jacob. Now Jacob has 12 sons. God promised to bring forth a great nation from Abraham.

How do you see God's plan for a family of his own beginning to unfold?

Younger children may need some help in seeing how the pieces are beginning to fit together.

Day 2

Today's discussion question can be extremely profound. Don't rush the conversation. Ask the Lord to help give your entire family insights into God's faithfulness on a very personal level.

Can you make a chart of your four great-grandfathers, your two grandfathers and your father?

How has God blessed your family through the generations?

Use a large sheet of paper or a whiteboard to make a chart. The children will be able to come up with parents and grandparents, but the adults will probably have to help fill in the blanks going back another generation or two. As you talk through today's question, children may be confused as they try to answer. Give them a jumpstart by telling them the story of how the Lord protected grandpa during the war, or saved grandma's life in the car wreck, or helped you and your spouse adopt a much-wanted child. As they get the concept, your children's minds may race as they begin to remember God's blessing in so many ways. This is a foundational truth that each of us needs to rehearse again and again: God's faithfulness and blessing in our lives.

Day 3

Read this week's "Watering the Seedling" from your *Firmly Planted* book. Every family has good people and some not-so-good people in it.

Do you think all 12 of Jacob's sons are going to turn out to be good people? Why?

Would it surprise you if all 12 were good men?

Thinking back on yesterday's discussion, you may recall one or more people in your own family history who made some serious mistakes. Help your children see that God's overall plan for your family was never ruined just because a few people were not perfect. God's promise to Abraham wasn't dependent on anyone else. God's promises are true because God Himself is True.

Day 4

Pray and thank the Lord for His insights this semester. Remind your children that learning the story of God is something we'll do for all eternity, not just 10 weeks. Next semester we'll see that some of Jacob's 12 sons were not good men. But we'll also see that God used them anyway.

Children often have a highly developed sense of fairness and they may be angry or confused that God can use or bless even people who make poor choices sometimes. This is a great time to discuss this important paradox: God can still use us even when we're not righteous. There are amazing blessings for those who try to make good and right choices in their lives.